Contents

1 Who is That Guy? 1

2 The Long Baseball Road 9

3 The Home Run Chase 19

4 The Race is On 25

5 Face to Face 41

6 Sammy Show-Biz 47

7 Pride of a Nation 53

8 The Businessman 67

Sammy Sosa's Quick Facts 75

Year-by-Year Summary 76

Career Highlights 77

Sammy Sosa's Home Run List 81

The author's scorecard for Sammy Sosa's historic 61st and 62nd home runs.

Sammy Sosa: Slammin' Sammy!

by

George Castle

Sports Publishing Inc.
www.SportsPublishingInc.com

Editor, Director of Production: Susan M. McKinney
Book design: Michelle R. Dressen
Book layout: Susan M. McKinney and Jennifer L. Polson
Cover design: Scot Muncaster

ISBN: 1-58261-029-0
Library of Congress Number: 98-89115

SPORTS PUBLISHING INC.
804 N. Neil
Champaign, IL 61820
www.SportsPublishingInc.com

Printed in the United States.

Front and back cover photos by Ron Vesely.

CHAPTER ONE

Who is That Guy?

When baseball fans talked about records that would never be broken, there always was one at the top of the list: Roger Maris' 61 home runs in the 1961 season.

The feeling was that no one—including Babe Ruth, Henry Aaron or Willie Mays—had hit that many in a season. How could anyone playing today ever do it?

Sure, Ken Griffey Jr. had come close. So had Mark McGwire. But getting close wasn't breaking the record. That was a record that would stand forever.

However, as the 1998 baseball season went from April to May to June, a funny thing happened. Some fans began wondering if this was the year when Maris' record would be broken. Griffey was hitting his usual number of early-season homers and McGwire had picked up where he left off in the 1997 season.

As June turned into July, a third name was added to the list of possible record breakers: Sammy Sosa. "Sammy who?" some fans asked. "You must be kidding," other fans said.

But Sammy Sosa wasn't laughing. Neither were his Chicago Cubs teammates or the fans in Wrigley Field. And neither were the pitchers in the National League. They knew who Sammy Sosa was.

He was the Cubs' right fielder who grew up in the Dominican Republic, part of an island in

CHICAGO CUBS vs. MILWAUKEE BREWERS
Wednesday, September 23, 1998

CHICAGO CUBS (88-70)

AVG.	HR	RBI	PLAYER	POS.	1	2	3	4	5	6	7	8	9	10	AB	R	H	RBI
.279	2	21	1-Lance Johnson	CF														
.258	23	74	18-Jose Hernandez	SS														
.312	17	89	17-Mark Grace	1B														
.303	63	154	21-Sammy Sosa	RF														
.376	8	23	6-Glenallen Hill	LF														
.280	18	66	8-Gary Gaetti *Alexander ss / 8th*	3B														
.301	8	53	12-Mickey Morandini	2B														
.222	7	35	9-Scott Servais	C														
.267	1	7	46-Steve Trachsel	RHP														

PITCHER	W	L	S	IP	H	R	ER	BB	SO	HB	WP	BK	HR
Steve Trachsel (14-8)				6⅓	6	4	4	1	4				
Heredia / 7th													
Karchner / 7th													
Beck / 9th													

SH —
SF —
SB —   CS —
DP —   HB —
GDP —

MILWAUKEE BREWERS (72-85)

A – 45,33

AVG.	HR	RBI	PLAYER	POS.	1	2	3	4	5	6	7	8	9	10	AB	R	H	RBI
.307	7	43	1-Fernando Vina	2B														
.320	6	52	8-Mark Loretta	1B														
.326	14	67	26-Jeff Cirillo	3B														
.263	38	124	20-Jeromy Burnitz	RF														
.269	8	58	9-Marquis Grissom	CF														
.232	9	28	5-Geoff Jenkins	LF														
.221	15	46	2-Jose Valentin	SS														
.240	9	28	33-Bobby Hughes	C														
.083	0	1	52-Rafael Roque *47 Reyes p / 5th*	LHP														

D. Jackson   Banks ph / 7th

Sammy hits Nos. 64 and 65.

the Caribbean Sea. Always smiling, always friendly, always playing hard, Sosa had a lot of fans in Chicago.

Even though he was not known as a home run hitter, he showed everyone what kind of power he had with 40 home runs in the 1996 season. However, 40 home runs is a long way from Maris' 61.

When it first was suggested that Sammy could approach the record, he shrugged it off. He told reporters that McGwire was "The Man" and the one who would have a shot at "The Record." Even as the season turned from July to August to September and McGwire and Sosa were neck-and-neck in the home run race, there was Smilin' Sammy, telling everyone how happy he was to play baseball and cheering for McGwire to hit another long ball.

Suddenly, McGwire also began to cheer for Sosa. And the public—in Chicago, St. Louis, the Dominican Republic, and every place where there

Friendly foes: Sammy Sosa and Mark McGwire.
(AP/Wide World Photos—Eric Draper)

was a TV or newspaper—began cheering for both players to challenge Maris' mark.

Despite the competition, a bonding took place between the two superstars and a friendship was formed. They genuinely liked each other. So, when both players began nearing No. 61, the entire nation was watching every swing by both players in every game.

There was Sosa, hitting one in Chicago, only to have McGwire match it in St. Louis. Finally, the Cubs and Cardinals squared off against each other on Labor Day weekend with the record within reach.

It was McGwire who got to 61 first. It was McGwire who wound up with 70 during the entire season. But Sosa got to 61, too (September 13 against the Milwaukee Brewers) and ended up with 66 home runs, second only to his good friend, McGwire. If it weren't for McGwire, Sosa would

Dominican superstar. (Photo by Ron Vesely)

be recognized as the greatest home run hitter in baseball history.

That suits Sosa just fine. His team continued to win ball games in the final month of the season and advanced to the National League Playoffs. That's why Sosa hit home runs—to help his team win games.

The Chicago Cubs were winners during the 1998 season. Mark McGwire was a winner in 1998. And Sammy Sosa was a winner, too.

The Long Baseball Road

Sammy Sosa advanced rapidly once he began playing organized baseball at 14. Helped by his older brother, Luis, he learned the game just in time to be signed by a local Dominican professional team run by Francisco Acevedo. By agreeing to play for Acevedo, Sosa would be brought to the attention of scouts for teams in the United States.

Acevedo fulfilled the agreement by contacting Omar Minaya of the Texas Rangers. Minaya

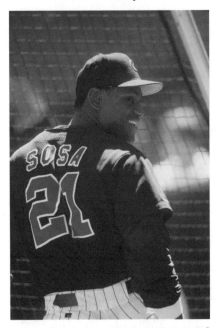

Sosa drew scouts' attention with his aggressiveness, vibrancy and enthusiasm. (Photo by Ron Vesely)

was a coach in the rookie-level Gulf Coast League in Florida. Minaya said that in 1985, only four teams — the Rangers, Los Angeles Dodgers, Toronto Blue Jays and Pittsburgh Pirates—were putting in a lot of time scouting players in the Domincan Republic.

Minaya had part-time scout Amado Dinzey check out Sosa. Dinzey reported that the kid was available to be signed, and Sosa was brought to a team tryout.

Other Rangers officials noticed Sosa at the tryout, simply because Sosa intended it to be that way. His street smarts enabled him to stand out from the crowd.

"The first thing that got your attention was his aggressiveness, vibrancy and enthusiasm," then-Rangers scouting director Sandy Johnson said. "It was as if he was saying, 'I can get these guys' attention.' He would not be denied about getting your attention. His mission was going to the tryout camp and getting signed that day. His body language was such that everything was at full speed.

"At this stage, he was 5-foot-10, 150 pounds, all arms and legs. He was like a young colt. He was not one of the faster ones; he didn't run a good time (in the 60-yard dash). He was very crude and kind of out of control, although in a good way. But he had some things going for him.

Chicago's No. 21 has a definite flair for the game. (Photo by Ron Vesely)

"He got in the batting cage, and even though he didn't smoke the ball or crush it, you saw he had tremendous aggressiveness and bat speed. He showed enough where you wanted to give him an opportunity. He had the flair.

"The only way Sammy Sosa knew how to get out of the Dominican was by swinging the bat. If he doesn't swing the bat, he's not going to get signed. He's not going to get a visa, he's not going to play in America."

Sosa, still just 16, signed for $3,500 on July 30, 1985 with the Rangers.

To prepare the Dominican players for moving to the U.S., the Rangers sent the kids to a baseball academy at the University of Santo Domingo. Sosa traveled 30 miles each way every day from San Pedro de Macoris. The trip on a local bus took 90 minutes.

"We gave him and the other young players meal money," Minaya said. "Whatever he'd get, he'd split with his family."

Sosa continued his attention-grabbing style when he played his first pro game in 1986 at Sarasota (Florida) of the Gulf Coast League. As a 17-year-old, Sosa batted .275.

In 1987, Sosa began attracting attention throughout the game at Gastonia (South Carolina) of the South Atlantic League. He led the team in batting (.279), games played (129), runs (73), hits

(145) and doubles (27). He also began showing flashes of power with 11 homers and 59 RBIs.

In 1988, the Rangers moved Sosa to Port Charlotte (Florida), a higher Class-A league.

"You knew he was going to play in the big leagues," said Bobby Jones, his manager. "His work ethic was outstanding; his hustle was outstanding. He was a hungry ballplayer and wanted it more than anyone else."

He batted just .229 with 106 strikeouts in 507 at-bats. But he also led the Florida State League with 12 triples and had his highest pro stolen base total, 42.

Sosa's days in the Rangers organization would come to a close in 1989. He had played 66 games at Class AA Tulsa when he got called up for a brief time to the big leagues.

Rangers General Manager Tom Grieve was the first person to give Sosa a chance to play in the

When Sammy Sosa was sixteen years old, he was signed by the Rangers for just $3,500. (Photo by Ron Vesely)

majors. Just 20, Sosa was called up to the Rangers on June 15 after batting .297 with Tulsa of the Texas League. Sosa barely had much Double-A experience, let alone any time in Triple-A. He was only playing in his fourth pro season.

"I think one of the things we fell victim to is promoting players at a young age before their experience in the minors warranted it," Grieve said. "We didn't have a lot of money (for veterans) at the big-league level, and this was what we could afford to do. We had a large group of very talented players in the minors."

Sosa's first big league game was on June 16, 1989 against the New York Yankees. Sosa had a single and double in four at-bats. Five days later, he slugged his first big-league homer off the Boston Red Sox' Roger Clemens at Fenway Park in Boston.

"I thought he had the right attitude," then-Rangers manager Bobby Valentine said. "I thought he'd have decent long-ball potential. Not big power, but maybe around 15 to 20 homers."

Despite his potential, on July 29, 1989, Sosa was traded by the Rangers with Wilson Alvarez to the Chicago White Sox for Harold Baines and Fred Monrigue.

Sosa enjoyed success as a White Sox. In two-plus seasons, he hit 28 home runs and had 52 stolen bases. However, he batted just .230.

The White Sox traded Sammy across town to the Chicago Cubs on March 30, 1992. He, along with pitcher Ken Patterson, went to the Sox for outfielder George Bell.

Sammy played in the minors for portions of six different seasons. (Photo by Ron Vesely)

Sosa suffered a broken right hand and a broken left ankle, limiting his playing time to 67 games in 1992. But when healthy, he produced his first 30-30 season in 1993, with 33 homers and 36 steals.

Sosa has stolen 217 bases in 10 major league seasons. (Photo by Ron Vesely)

In 1994, he batted .300 and had 25 home runs; in '95 he had 36 homers and 119 RBIs; in '96 he had 40 home runs; and in '97 he had 36 homers.

That set the stage for the memorable 1998 season.

The Home Run Chase

Sammy Sosa's locker was not what you would expect from a superstar.

Several years ago Sosa had a photo of Roberto Clemente in the locker, but that's gone, replaced by a photo of wife Sonia and their four children. A box of Flintstones vitamins, a prop he'd used for comic effect in 1998, and a bottle of Ginseng Gold were on the top shelf. There was an extra, unused locker cubicle next door, a privilege often given to a top star.

Sammy's historic 20-homer in June kept him in the race with Mark McGwire. (Photo by Ron Vesely)

Three hours before games, Sosa and locker mate Jose Hernandez would sit side by side, dressing, talking softly. Sosa spent a couple of minutes each time slapping talcum powder on his legs and thighs before he pulled on his uniform pants for batting practice. He also used this time to attend to filling out names for tickets or passes, signing autographs, engaging in a bit of horseplay with teammates.

Cell phones permit last-minute conversations with loved ones and business associates, and Sosa sometimes jumped on the phone. Off the line, he'd wander halfway down the clubhouse to sit with fellow Dominican players Manny Alexander, Sandy Martinez and Henry Rodriguez, whose lockers were all clustered. That was his form of relaxation as the first pitch neared, and he'd continue that pattern even as his home run total climbed into the 60s.

But on July 1, 1998, Sosa still could not have imagined his journey into the record books, despite his historic 20-homer June, despite the fans' expectations. The Cubs had their ups and downs at this point.

"We're winning together and staying together," he said. "We know we can go out and play good against anyone. I'm really happy now. I go home at night and can sleep. We pick each other up. Let's be happy now because everything's going great."

Sosa would not homer in the next three games, all Cubs victories, as the All-Star break loomed. He was human, after all. And on the morning of July 5, a chill went through Cubdom when Sosa was scratched from the Cubs lineup for the game against the Pittsburgh Pirates at Wrigley Field. That would turn out to be the fourth and final game he would miss all season.

Sosa's left shoulder was stiff; he claimed he had slept wrong the night before. He'd have to miss his second All-Star Game. Sosa still showed up in Denver to partake in ceremonies, sign autographs and clown around in the dugout.

"I can't play, but I want to represent Chicago," he said. "Was I disappointed? Yes. But it's much better for this to happen to me now with three days' rest coming."

Sosa had gone into the All-Star break with 33 homers, four behind Mark McGwire and two behind Ken Griffey Jr.

En route to 66 rounds trippers, Sosa had collected 55 home runs through August 31, 1998. (Photo by Ron Vesely)

The Race is On

Having enjoyed the hoopla of the All-Star Game and with his shoulder soreness gone, he jumped back into the lineup for a four-game series against the Milwaukee Brewers at County Stadium starting July 9. Sosa slugged No. 34 against Jeff Juden during a 12-9 Cubs loss on July 9. The next night, he came back with No. 35, also in the second, off Scott Karl.

But now his pace of power slowed, even as the Cubs' pace of winning picked up. Sosa would

Slammin' Sammy and Big Mac (left) chat during a meeting at first base. (Photo by Ron Vesely)

not hit another homer for a whole week. Not until another week passed did Sosa really seem to energize himself for a real duel with McGwire. That took place in an unlikely location—at Bank One Ballpark in Phoenix. Sosa would take a long-time monkey off his back, and launched himself into direct competition with the St. Louis slugger.

Sosa had a big hole in his game with the bases loaded. He had belted 245 homers going into the first game of a four-game series against the Diamondbacks on July 27. None had ever come with the bases loaded.

Against the D-Backs' Willie Blair, Sosa warmed up with a two-run shot in the sixth inning. Two innings later, with the bases loaded, he broke the 4,428 at-bat spell with a long shot to center field off Alan Embree. A thrilled Sosa had to contain himself from dancing around the bases. He ended up driving in all the runs, reaching the 100

Sosa and McGwire (right) were National League teammates during the 1998 All-Star Game. (AP/Wide World Photos—Beth A. Keiser)

mark for the fourth consecutive season, in the Cubs' 6-2 victory.

"I'm not going to lie to you," Sosa said. "I'm not going to hear about that (bases-loaded failures) anymore, and it feels great.

"I'm sure he's glad he got that monkey off his back. It was a fluke thing," Cubs manager Jim Riggleman said.

But to ensure the grand slam was no fluke in and of itself, Sosa came through again the next night with a fifth-inning grand slam off Bob Wolcott into the packed left field seats. Now he recorded the first of numerous entries into the Cubs' record book— the first player in team history to slug grand slams in consecutive games (and the 18th major-leaguer overall to accomplish the feat). And he set a season high with his 41st homer.

Two months remained. Two good months of power, not sensational, just no long dry spells,

Mark McGwire (right) blows a trademark Sammy Sosa kiss to the Chicago slugger as the two meet at Wrigley Field. (AP/Wide World Photos—John Gaps III)

and Sosa could reach the Roger Maris record. But first, he had to contend with McGwire.

Strangely, the two sluggers began a kind of communication with one another during their interviews. McGwire suddenly loosened up a bit as August commenced, while Sosa began deferring to the red-bearded giant as "The Man," turning back all suggestions that he could break the Maris record and beat out McGwire for the home-run crown.

"It's excellent for the game," McGwire said of the race. "It's fantastic. I totally realize that. I think everyone realizes the game is on a rise now."

McGwire's own mid-season power lull enabled Sosa to creep up on him in their first head-to-head duel from August 7 to 9 at Busch Stadium in St. Louis. In a nationally televised game on Saturday afternoon, August 8, both sluggers and their teams displayed what true entertainment really was as they continued to revive baseball.

McGwire ended a 29 at-bat homerless drought, his longest of the season, with a homer in the fourth. Sosa saved his blast for when it really counted. With the Cubs trailing 5-3 and two outs in the ninth, he connected off Rick Croushore to tie it up. Tyler Houston slugged a two-run homer in the top of the 11th to give the Cubs a 7-5 lead.

But after an error by Jeff Blauser on a Brian Jordan grounder in the bottom of the 11th, Ray Lankford slugged a two-out, game-tying homer off Rod Beck after striking out in each of his previous five at-bats. Sosa then showed off his all-fields hitting style with an RBI single to right to put the Cubs ahead 8-7 in the top of the 12th. Cardinals catcher Eli Marrero answered that with a homer off Beck in the bottom of the 12th to make it 8-8. Lankford finally ended the wild affair with an RBI single in the bottom of the 13th.

McGwire would hit only one more homer in the next week, while Sosa slugged three, including two in one game on August 10 against the Giants. Now for the real big show—both tied at 47 going into the night of Tuesday, August 18 at Wrigley Field.

But both Sosa and McGwire struck out three times apiece as the Cubs won, 4-1.

Sosa finally pulled ahead for the first time in the home-run race in the fifth inning the next afternoon. He launched a two-run homer (No. 48) in the fifth off ex-Cub Kent Bottenfield. But Sammy's edge lasted less than an hour. McGwire tied him and the game with a solo shot onto Waveland Avenue off Matt Karchner in the eighth. In the 10th, the situation might have called for lefty Cubs reliever Terry Mulholland to pitch around McGwire with nobody on base. Servais confirmed that was the battle plan: "We didn't execute the

Sammy stares down the pitcher. (Photo by Ron Vesely)

pitch." Mulholland got too much of the plate with one pitch and McGwire got too much of the ball. No. 49 gave the Cardinals the lead, Lankford followed with another homer, and they eventually won 8-6.

That blast seemed to touch off a McGwire home-run binge, and Sosa gamely tried to keep up. He collected No. 49 two days later against Orel Hershiser of the San Francisco Giants. Then, on Sunday, August 23, Sosa's two-homer performance allowed him to reach and pass the 50 mark. Sosa became only the second Cub ever and the first Latin player to reach 50 with a fifth-inning blast.

After the game, word came that McGwire stayed ahead with his 53rd homer in Pittsburgh.

"He's 'The Man,'" Sosa said. "He's the type who can hit five, six homers in a couple of days. I put my money on him. I'm not thinking about the record. I'm coming here thinking about the game. If I think about the game, I'll play better."

Sammy Sosa is a ball-hawking right fielder ... (Photo by Ron Vesely)

... and has an excellent arm, too. (Photo by Ron Vesely)

Sosa tried to do that and came away with four more homers from August 26 to 31 as the Cubs won five of six from the Cincinnati Reds and Colorado Rockies. On Monday night, August 31, Sosa collected No. 55 in the third inning off Brett Tomko at Wrigley Field, tying McGwire once again. Tomko also had surrendered No. 52 five days previously in Cincinnati.

McGwire, of course, wasn't far from his mind.

"The reason I say he's 'The Man' is because every time we tie he jumps up there right away," Sosa said. "I was tied for about six hours. After that—boom!—he's back on top. I'm happy for him. He seems real happy. The last few interviews he has been enjoying it, and that's what you have to do. If you do that, it's going to be easier for him."

Sosa belted Nos. 56 and 57, keeping the heat on McGwire. But McGwire came through again, not wasting any time. He connected for No. 60 in the first inning off Reds lefty Dennis Reyes, tying Babe Ruth's best. "Let's just accept what is happening," he said. "Enjoy it. Ride the wave."

Not discouraged, Sosa belted yet another homer to right field. No. 58 came on a 3-and-1 pitch by Pirates lefty Sean Lawrence in the sixth inning. He was pumping 'em out almost as fast as in June. The blast was Sosa's ninth homer in 13 games.

"To me, I'm a winner already," he said. "I've gone so far this year and a lot more (home runs) are going to come. To me, just being behind Mark McGwire is being a winner."

He couldn't wait until he got to St. Louis.

"People have been waiting for this moment," Sosa said. "It's going to be tremendous. I'm sure they'd like to see Mark and I together for the last

Sosa had several memorable moments against the Cardinals in 1998. (Photo by Ron Vesely)

time this year . . . I'm willing to have a good time, like always."

Sosa had one more chance to close the gap before the Labor Day matchup. But he went 2-for-5, both singles, as the Cubs lost to the Pirates.

In addition to his 66 home runs in 1998, Sammy Sosa batted in a league-leading 158 RBIs. (Photo by Ron Vesely)

CHAPTER FIVE

Face to Face

September 7 opened with a nationally televised pregame press conference with both Sosa and McGwire. Both men enjoyed each other's company, both laughed it up, and Sosa hammed it up. "Baseball's been berry, berry good to me," Sammy blurted out without warning, cracking up McGwire and the audience. That would truly start a final month of belly laughs from the newest comic sensation wearing No. 21 in blue pinstripes.

McGwire wasted no time in providing the hot afternoon's drama. He connected for a 430-foot drive to left on a 1-and-1 pitch from the Cubs' Mike Morgan in the first inning. The media had a field day with the symmetry—the 61st homer came on McGwire's father John's 61st birthday. And, suddenly, McGwire invoked references to higher powers.

"Hopefully, the day that I die I can, after seeing the Lord, I can go see him and Babe Ruth and talk to them," he said.

Sosa applauded the homer from his station in right field, tapping his right hand into his gloved left. He hugged McGwire when he reached first on his solitary single. But he also struck out three times, including with the tying run on third and two out in the ninth in the Cardinals' 3-2 victory.

But all the while, the St. Louis crowd of 50,530 gave Sosa rousing ovations for each of his at-bats. That would continue the next night as both sluggers continued their duel.

The Cubs and Sosa could hardly concentrate on the concept of the wild-card race in the circus atmosphere enveloping McGwire. A World Series-sized contingent of more than 700 media members was in attendance, and the pack threatened to trample one another to get close to McGwire and Sosa. They got their wish on September 8. Steve Trachsel's worst scenario came true on his first pitch in the fourth, which McGwire blasted on a line just 341 feet over the left-field wall, his shortest, yet most memorable, homer of the season. Just as Trachsel figured, the game stopped. "There's nothing cool about it," Trachsel later said, but he was a majority of one. His Cubs infielders congratulated McGwire as he toured the bases. And, after hugging his son and jumping into the stands to greet the children of Roger Maris, McGwire held court in ceremonies near home plate.

The bear hug that warmed the hearts of baseball fans everywhere. (AP/Wide World Photos—James A. Finley)

Sosa at first hesitated, then ran in from right field. He leaped into McGwire's arms. McGwire gave him a bear hug and twirled Sosa around in his arms like he was a kid. The pair gave each other Sosa's trademark heart-taps.

"When he hugged me, it was a great moment I am not going to forget," Sosa said.

Later in the Cardinals' 6-3 victory, Sosa and McGwire talked at first base when Sammy reached on a single.

"I said to him," Sammy said, "'Maybe you can go home now and relax and take it easy and wait for me.'"

Sosa didn't catch McGwire. But he did belt 66 homers before the season was over. That's the second highest total in major league history. In addition, Sosa led the Cubs into postseason play.

Sammy's speed and hustle makes him a threat on the base paths. (Photo by Ron Vesely)

Sammy Show-Biz

Bit by bit, Sammy Sosa's personality was constructed from the late 1980s on, when he began learning about life in America as a Rangers' minor-leaguer and a young White Sox player. Just as he did on the field, developing from natural talent, Sosa came a long, long way with his personality and confidence in his life. And his ability to wise-crack in English was nothing short of amazing, mastering one-liners in a language he only began learning 10 years before.

Sammy Sosa passes out Dominican cigars in the Cubs locker room after Chicago's wild card race tie-breaking victory over San Francisco. (AP/Wide World Photos—Mike Fisher)

Sosa immediately responded to the almost-always adoring Cubs fans. "It's like I've been here all my life," he said in the spring of 1992. He began saluting the fans in the right field bleachers before every game, earning their support. That's a practice that continues today, and Sosa gave the right field bleacher bums a champagne shower on September 29, 1998, after he and the Cubs beat the San Francisco Giants, 5-3, in the wild-card tiebreaker game.

More importantly, a Sosa autograph became a collector's item at Wrigley Field. He became one of a few Cubs to go outside the parking lot after games to sign. Sosa also signed after batting practice, and several times was spotted sitting atop the dugout roof signing before games.

"The fans are right behind me," Sosa said. "They support me a lot, and that's why I take a lot of time to sign. They know I want to stay here. I will do anything to prove I want to stay here. This is where I got the opportunity to play. This is where people love me."

By that time, he had settled down with his second wife, Sonia, and began starting his family that eventually would grow to four children: Keysha, Kenia, Sammy, Jr. and Michael.

"When I am at the ballpark, I'm a baseball player," he said. "When I'm at home, I'm a family man."

Sonia couldn't often bring the children out to games. "It's a problem now a little bit," she said. "Little babies. The oldest is only five years old."

Sonia helped him after tough days at the plate.

"I tried to," she said. "He came to the house after a bad day. I tried to say only, 'Don't worry about that because they just sometimes happen. This is the game. So don't worry about today. Worry about tomorrow because tomorrow is better. It's important to you. Today's already happened, so don't worry about today. Just get better and think about what you can do, and you can do it better tomorrow.'"

Says Sammy, "When I am at the ballpark, I'm a baseball player. When I'm at home, I'm a family man." (Photo by Ron Vesely)

The classic stroke of Sammy Sosa. (Photo by Ron Vesely)

CHAPTER SEVEN

Pride of a Nation

Sammy Sosa was many things to many people in 1998.

But to the 8 million citizens of the Dominican Republic, his homeland, he was everything. He was a hero during the great home run chase. He was a spokesman to show his people love a laugh like anyone else. And he was a family man, showing his love for his wife, children, mother, brothers and sisters almost daily.

In the end, though, he was a giver in time of need. Most Dominicans in the poor eastern two-

Lucrecia Sosa admires a painting of her son, Sammy, in her home in San Pedro de Macoris, Dominican Republic. (AP/Wide World Photos— Milton Gonzalez)

thirds of the Caribbean island of Hispaniola the country shares with an even poorer Haiti had few possessions to lose in time of disaster. The worst-case situation, though, took place in late September 1998. Hurricane Georges hit the Dominican head on, killing hundreds, leaving thousands homeless, and destroying 90 percent of the main cash crops upon which the country depends. Authorities in the capital of Santo Domingo did not open shelters until after strong winds and rain had hit the city.

Sosa had given so much to his family and people ever since he signed his first pro baseball contract and sent his dollars back home to his mother, Lucrecia. He put his own money back into the country, building a shopping plaza, opening a baseball school at which the players were housed and fed, and started a Christmas-present donation fund for kids.

Sosa's celebrity and ability to help his native people was never more needed than when the hurricane ripped through the island. He quickly created a Sammy Sosa Foundation with the Cubs to send donations of money and supplies to the Dominican. Sosa and teammates Henry Rodriguez and Manny Alexander went to the Dominican consulate in Houston after the September 26 game to help load supplies for shipment. United Parcel Service even donated a plane to send about $35,000 in supplies to Santo Domingo.

"I've been working hard to raise money and do what I can for my country," Sosa said. "It's not about home runs. It's about human beings back in my country. They have nothing. A lot of people are dying and have no homes and no food. It's a tough situation."

Said Bernardo Vega, Dominican ambassador to the United States, "As far as I'm concerned, he's the real Dominican ambassador. I just shuffle papers."

"It's unbelievable," said Cubs outfielder Henry Rodriguez, a native of Santo Domingo. "I grew up in a really poor area. My family was poor and we shared. Shared everything. Even with other poor people, they come and ask for something, a piece of bread or whatever, and we share."

Dominicans have the Catholic church as a backbone through the poverty that produces an annual income of less than $1,500 a person.

"We're religious people," said Omar Minaya, the Rangers scout who signed Sosa in 1985, who now is the highest-ranking Hispanic baseball executive in the game as assistant general manager of the New York Mets.

"The church provide a lot of discipline," Minaya said. "The humbleness of the people comes from the church. It teaches humbleness, goodness and sharing."

Fans in Sammy Sosa's hometown of San Pedro de Macoris react as their idol goes to bat in the season finale versus Houston. Amid the destruction of Hurricane Georges, which left many with no power, telephones or running water, hundreds of people scrambled to find places to see or hear Sosa's final regular-season game. (AP/Wide World Photos— Jose Luis Magana)

Such an environment can't kill dreams. The fondest of dreams are turned into reality by hundreds of Dominican teenagers who have signed pro baseball contracts in recent decades. If baseball used to be America's pastime, it is the Dominican Republic's passion, a way off the island for the boys playing on rocky fields, using milk cartons for gloves, broomsticks for bats, and rolled-up whatevers for baseballs. Bottle caps make great ball substitutes; they dive and dip and simulate tricky curve balls for the young hitters.

More than 40 Dominicans play Major League Baseball, including 10 from San Pedro de Macoris, a city of 90,000 people and a 90-minute drive east of Santo Domingo. George Bell, Julio Franco and Alfredo Griffin hail from San Pedro, all played on a rough field nicknamed "Mexico" by the locals. Sammy Sosa got his start there, too.

Members of Sammy's family, including his mother Lucrecia (at right in white dress), and other honored guests, applaud their hero. (Photo by Ron Vesely)

Sammy was one of six children of Bautista and Lucrecia Montero. His brothers and sisters are Luis, 36; Sonia, 35; Juan, 34; Raquel, 32; and Jose, 24. Sosa's father, Bautista Moreno, died when Sammy was 7.

"She deserves all the credit," Rodriguez said of Lucrecia Sosa. "To raise six kids in the whole family, I think it takes a lot of hard work, a lot of energy, a lot of crying and seeing that you could not afford to buy a pair of shoes for each of your kids. She deserves everything. Whatever, I don't think there's enough words to describe what she did. She did everything. It's unbelievable."

Although Lucrecia would remarry, change the family name to Sosa and add stepsons Carlos and Nani to the family, the kids had to go out and help support the household. The young Sosa followed in the path of so many San Pedro de Macoris boys, shining shoes in a centrally-located plaza area called the Parque Duarte.

It was there that Sammy Sosa got his first break that started him on the path toward 66 homers, 158 RBIs and status as a sports hero.

Massachusetts native Bill Chase had arrived in San Pedro de Macoris in 1979 to start a shoe factory.

"Dominicans are excellent workers with excellent hands," Chase said. "Having a job meant something to them. They didn't mind repetitive work, and were orderly. At one point I had 1,500 workers, and I can't ever remember where we had a fight."

Chase scouted out San Pedro de Macoris upon his arrival. His life—and that of the little kid he would meet—was about to change.

"The first night in town, I didn't know the area well, I go down to the town square, and there are 200 kids shining shoes," Chase recalled. One local resident knew two of the kids: Sammy and Juan Sosa. He pointed them out to Chase, telling him they were nice kids.

"They shined my shoes," he said. "Every night, I'd go to the square and just watch everybody, and the kids shined my shoes. Sammy had that big smile; a lot of the kids do."

Chase continued to go to Parque Duarte for his shoe shines. Then he began going to a diner named Restaurant 29. The Sosa kids figured out Chase's habits, and began waiting for him at the restaurant, earning a peso a shine.

But Sammy and his brother didn't stop there. They found out where Chase and wife Debbie lived. By now Sammy was joined by little brother Jose, who was too young to shine shoes.

"They were likable kids," Chase said. "They knew how to get to your heart. Jose wasn't shining shoes. He would entertain me, do handstands. I'd give him some pesos for that."

One day Debbie Chase took a bite of a locally grown apple. "She didn't like it, and the boys asked if they could give it to their mama," Chase said. Debbie Chase began to buy the Sosa boys clothes and other items, while her husband let them hang around the shoe factory when they weren't attending school. Chase's customers were given shoe shines, and thus Lucrecia Sosa sometimes found her sons bringing home $5 bills; that was a king's ransom in the Dominican. With indoor plumbing a luxury in San Pedro, the Sosa boys took weekend showers at the factory.

"They have trenches and outhouses," Chase said. "They'd take empty cement drums and let rain water collect in them. That was their showers."

Sosa was so busy working that he didn't play baseball regularly. Luis Sosa, who had played, got his brother started in the game in an organized fashion at 14. Chase bought him his first real glove.

Sosa did not at first impress as a player. "I never thought he'd turn out like this. He was a mediocre player," David de la Cruz, now manager of Sosa's baseball school team, said.

But the young Sosa knew what to do to impress Rangers scouts in his 1985 tryout. His mother was overjoyed when he signed.

Sammy sent about 90 percent of his pay as a low minor-leaguer back to his mother. McDonald's was his usual restaurant choice in America.

"When the paychecks ran out after the season, he had the winter to get through," Chase said of the off-seasons of the late 1980s. He loaned Sosa money to get him through. After Sosa finally made it to the White Sox, he was so happy he wanted to buy Lucrecia Sosa a house. Sosa now made good money as a big leaguer, but the home still cost $50,000. Again, Chase came through.

"I think when you buy a present for your mom, it doesn't have to be a house," the Cubs' Rodriguez said. "It doesn't have to be a car. They appreciate anything because it comes from one of the kids. I bought a house for my mom. My mom is crazy about that. And not because of the house itself, but because I bought it. It's really amazing how mothers react when their kids bring to the house a piece of bread or whatever. They feel so proud because you're her kid."

CHAPTER EIGHT

The Businessman

Sosa's salary finally rose into the million dollar range with the Cubs in the mid-1990s. He took care of his family and bought himself a nice four-bedroom home in a Santo Domingo neighborhood. More importantly, he began investing in his own country.

In 1996, he and Chase began building 30-30 Plaza, a $1.2-million project named for his 30-homer, 30-stolen base season. The three-story combination of offices and shops near Parque Duarte surrounds a statue of Sosa in the courtyard.

"A lot of people, when they get a lot of money, they throw it away," Sosa said. "They forget about tomorrow. I'm not trying to do this. I know I'm not going to play forever. Someday I'll have to pack up and come home.

Sosa was loyal to his country long before he was needed to organize hurricane relief.

"I'll never forget where I came from," he said. "I'm proud of the United States. They've given me everything that I have. They gave me the opportunity to be Sammy Sosa today. But I have to remember that these are my people, people I have to take care of, people I have to give jobs to when I opened the plaza. This is my life."

Sosa did not stop with 30-30 Plaza, though. He created a Sammy Sosa baseball school in San Pedro. The players take the field with the name "Sosa" on their jerseys. Sosa feeds and houses the players, buys their equipment and pays the salaries of the employees. Best of all, he gives hope where none might have existed.

By 1998, Sosa was giving away about $500,000 a year out of his own pocket. He bought 250 computers for Dominican schools.

Chase began a foundation that swung into action with hurricane relief. He also advised Sosa on the endorsement deals that came his way as his home run totals mounted.

With competition from other Caribbean resort areas, the Dominican Republic is trying to build up its tourist industry. Sosa can't do anything but help, while improving the image of Dominicans in the United States.

"He's doing more for our country than our tourist board to show it's worth visiting," said Vega. "Among certain people there was a notion that Dominicans were people of violence, that they were into drugs and illegal migrants. What Sammy is showing is what the average Dominican is.

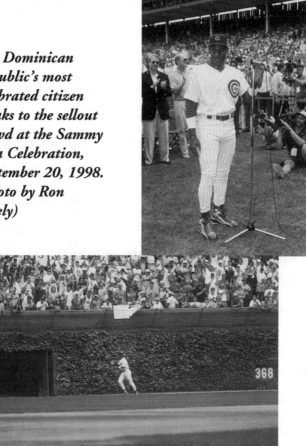

The Dominican Republic's most celebrated citizen speaks to the sellout crowd at the Sammy Sosa Celebration, September 20, 1998. (Photo by Ron Vesely)

With the theme from "Superman" blaring over the loudspeakers, Sammy takes a victory trot around Wrigley Field. (Photo by Ron Vesely)

"I was giving a speech to a group of American investors and I wasn't getting much applause," Vega said. "But the moment I mentioned Sammy Sosa, everybody applauded. I took the opportunity to explain about his hometown. It just transformed from an old backwater to an expanding city with a lot of free trade zones. Now we are the fourth biggest supplier to the United States of clothes and apparel. The No. 1 supplier of sugar and cigars. The sixth biggest supplier of shoes.

"Essentially, we live from tourism and all these assembly plants for exporting."

Sosa has become a hero at home on and off the field. Even with the hurricane, without electricity or access to TV and radios, Dominicans went to great lengths to find out news of Sosa's feats as the 1998 regular-season wound down. They asked visiting Americans, who possessed the ultimate prize—satellite trucks that could connect to the latest news about Sosa.

Prior to the disaster, the country practically shut down during Cubs telecasts. Sosa's games were tape-delayed for late broadcast in the Dominican for four seasons. But on September 1, 1998, just after Sosa slugged his 55th homer, a complete Dominican TV crew took over a Wrigley Field press box booth to show the games live back home.

"People in offices had problems because their employees watched the games," said broadcaster Jose Ravel of Deportes En La Cumbre, the Dominican Sports Broadcasting Co. "They don't work. But most of the offices ended up bringing in a TV."

Ravel created excitement with a lot of home run calls. A typical Sosa homer was described back to the Dominican in Spanish as: *Batazo largo, grande la bola se va y la saco. Sammy Sosa. Bay Bay Charley.* In English: "Long drive, big, the ball is going, and it's out. Sammy Sosa. Bye, Bye Charley."

Not even a hurricane can sweep away the good feeling of Sammy Sosa—pride of a little country. The faith and hope of proud people toward their favorite son was best described by Julia Sosa, Sammy's 80-year-old grandmother.

"The things God does are big," she said.

Sosa congratulates Mickey Morandini following a Cubs victory. (Photo by Ron Vesely)

Sammy Sosa. (Photo by Ron Vesely)

Sammy Sosa's
Quick Facts

Full Name: *Samuel Sosa*
Team: *Chicago Cubs*
Hometown: *San Pedro, Dominican Republic*
Position: *Outfielder*
Jersey Number: *21*
Bats: *Right*
Throws: *Right*
Height: *6-0*
Weight: *190 pounds*
Birthdate: *Nov. 12, 1968*

1998 Highlight: *Named National League's Most Valuable Player*

Stats Spotlight: *Hit 66 homers in 1998, second-most in Major League Baseball History*

Little-known Fact: *Sixteen-year-old Sammy Sosa signed his first contract for $3,500*

Year-by-Year Summary

Year	Club	Avg.	G	AB	HR	RBI	SB
1986	Gulf Coast (rookie)	.275	61	229	4	28	11
1987	Gastonia (A)	.279	129	519	11	59	22
1988	Port Charlotte (A)	.229	131	507	9	51	42
1989	Tulsa (AA)	.297	66	273	7	31	16
	Texas	.238	25	84	1	3	0
	Oklahoma City (AAA)	.103	10	39	4		
	Vancouver (AAA)	.367	13	49	1	5	3
	White Sox	.273	33	99	3	10	7
1990	White Sox	.233	153	532	15	70	32
1991	White Sox	.203	116	316	10	33	13
	Vancouver (AAA)	.267	32	116	3	19	9
1992	Cubs	.260	67	262	8	25	15
	Iowa	.316	5	19	0	1	5
1993	Cubs	.261	159	598	33	93	36
1994	Cubs	.300	105	426	25	70	22
1995	Cubs	.268	144	564	36	119	34
1996	Cubs	.273	124	498	40	100	18
1997	Cubs	.251	162	642	36	119	22
1998	Cubs	.308	158	643	66	158	18
Major League Total		.264	1247	4664	273	800	217

Career Highlights
1989-1997

- Slugged first homer off Boston Red Sox' Roger Clemens on June 21, 1989 at Fenway Park as a Texas Ranger

- Belted a homer in a 3-for-3 night in White Sox debut on August 22, 1989 against the Minnesota Twins at Metrodome

- Only American League player to rank in double figures in doubles (26), triples (10) and homers (15) in 1990

- Hit first Cubs homer May 7, 1992 against the Houston Astros' Ryan Bowen

- Went 6-for-6, completing a nine straight hit performance, on July 2, 1993 against the Colorado Rockies at Mile High Stadium in Denver

In 1993, Sammy became the first Cub ever to hit 30 home runs and steal 30 bases in the same season. (Photo by Ron Vesely)

- Became first Cub ever to hit 30 homers and steal 30 bases with theft of second in sixth inning against San Francisco Giants at Candlestick Park on September 15, 1993

- Had career-high 17 outfield assists in 1993, ranking second in National League and most by a Cub since Lou Brock in 1963

- Named to the National League All-Star team for the first time in 1995, going 0-for-1 in Midsummer Classic at Ballpark at Arlington

- Slugged 10 homers in a 13-game span from August 17 to August 29, 1995

- After finishing tied for second in homers (36) and second in RBIs (119) in NL, named to league's post-season *Sporting News* all-star team

- Became first player to belt two homers in one inning on May 16, 1996 against the Houston Astros, leading off the seventh with a solo shot off Jeff Tabaka and adding a two-run blast off Jim Dougherty later in the inning

- Recorded his first career three-homer game on June 5, 1996 against the Philadelphia Phillies at Wrigley Field

- Selected as NL Player of the Month for July 1996 after a 10-homer, 29-RBI, .358 performance

- Was leading NL with 40 homers on August 20, 1996 when a pitch by the Florida Marlins' Mark Hutton broke his right hand in a game at Wrigley Field

- Set a career single-game high with six RBIs with a homer and triple on May 16, 1997 against the San Diego Padres

- Slashed first inside-the-park homer in career on May 26, 1997 in the sixth inning off the Pirates' Francisco Cordova at Three Rivers Stadium

Sammy Sosa's
Home Run List

The following is a list of Sammy Sosa's home runs in
1998:

HR	Date	Inning	Location	Pitcher	Inning	Runners	Direction
1	April 4	5	Montreal	Marc Valdes	3	solo	RF
2	April 11	11	At Montreal	Anthony Telford	7	solo	RF
3	April 15	14	At New York	Dennis Cook	8	solo	LF
4	April 23	21	San Diego	Dan Miceli	9	solo	CF
5	April 24	22	At Los Angeles	Ismael Valdes	1	solo	CF
6	April 27	25	At San Diego	Joey Hamilton	1	two-run	CF
7	May 3	30	St Louis	Cliff Politte	1	solo	LF
8	May 16	42	At Cincinnati	Scott Sullivan	3	three-run	CF
9	May 22	47	At Atlanta	Greg Maddux	1	solo	CF
10	May 25	50	At Atlanta	Kevin Millwood	4	solo	RF
11	May 25	50	At Atlanta	Mike Cather	8	solo	CF
12	May 27	51	Philadelphia	Darrin Winston	8	solo	LF
13	May 27	51	Philadelphia	Wayne Gomes	9	two-run	LF
14	June 1	56	Florida	Ryan Dempster	1	two-run	LF
15	June 1	56	Florida	Oscar Henriquez	8	three-run	CF
16	June 3	58	Florida	Livan Hernandez	5	two-run	LF
17	June 5	59	White Sox	Jim Parque	5	two-run	RF
18	June 6	60	White Sox	Carlos Castillo	7	solo	CF
19	June 7	61	White Sox	James Baldwin	5	three-run	CF
20	June 8	62	At Minnesota	LaTroy Hawkins	3	solo	RF
21	June 13	66	At Philadelphia	Mark Portugal	6	two-run	RF
22	June 15	68	Milwaukee	Cal Eldred	1	solo	RF
23	June 15	68	Milwaukee	Cal Eldred	3	solo	LF
24	June 15	68	Milwaukee	Cal Eldred	7	solo	CF
25	June 17	70	Milwaukee	Bronswell Patrick	4	solo	LF
26	June 19	72	Philadelphia	Carlton Loewer	1	solo	LF

27	June 19	72	Philadelphia	Carlton Loewer	1	solo	LF
28	June 20	73	Philadelphia	Matt Beach	3	two-run	LF
29	June 20	73	Philadelphia	Toby Borland	6	three-run	LF
30	June 21	74	Philadelphia	Tyler Green	4	solo	RF
31	June 24	77	At Detroit	Seth Greisinger	1	solo	LF
32	June 25	78	At Detroit	Brian Moehler	7	solo	RF
33	June 30	82	Arizona	Alan Embree	8	solo	RF
34	July 9	88	At Milwaukee	Jeff Juden	2	two-run	CF
35	July 10	89	At Milwaukee	Scott Karl	2	solo	LF
36	July 17	95	At Florida	Kirt Ojala	6	two-run	CF
37	July 22	100	Montreal	Miguel Batista	8	three-run	RF
38	July 26	105	New York	Rick Reed	6	two-run	CF
39	July 27	106	At Arizona	Willie Blair	6	two-run	RF
40	July 27	106	At Arizona	Alan Embree	8	grand slam	CF
41	July 28	107	At Arizona	Bob Wolcott	5	grand slam	LF
42	July 31	110	Colorado	Jamey Wright	1	solo	RF
43	August 5	115	Arizona	Andy Benes	3	two-run	LF
44	August 8	117	At St. Louis	Rick Croushore	9	two-run	LF
45	August 10	119	At San Francisco	Russ Ortiz	5	solo	LF
46	August 10	119	At San Francisco	Chris Brock	7	solo	CF
47	August 16	124	At Houston	Sean Bergman	4	solo	RF
48	August 19	126	St. Louis	Kent Bottenfield	5	two-run	LF
49	August 21	128	San Francisco	Orel Hershiser	5	two-run	CF
50	August 23	130	Houston	Jose Lima	5	solo	LF
51	August 23	130	Houston	Jose Lima	8	solo	LF
52	August 26	133	At Cincinnati	Brett Tomko	3	solo	LF
53	August 28	135	At Colorado	John Thompson	1	solo	RF
54	August 30	137	At Colorado	Darryl Kile	1	two-run	LF
55	August 31	138	Cincinnati	Brett Tomko	3	two-run	LF
56	September 2	140	Cincinnati	Jason Bere	6	solo	RF
57	September 4	141	At Pittsburgh	Jason Schmidt	1	solo	RF
58	September 5	142	At Pittsburgh	Sean Lawrence	6	solo	RF
59	September 11	148	Milwaukee	Bill Pulsipher	5	solo	RF
60	September 12	149	Milwaukee	Valerio De Los Santos	7	three-run	LF
61	September 13	150	Milwaukee	Bronswell Patrick	5	two-run	LF
62	September 13	150	Milwaukee	Eric Plunk	9	solo	LF
63	September 16	153	At San Diego	Brian Boehringer	8	grand slam	LF
64	September 23	158	At Milwaukee	Rafael Roque	5	solo	RF
65	September 23	158	At Milwaukee	Rod Henderson	6	solo	CF
66	September 25	159	At Houston	Jose Lima	4	solo	LF

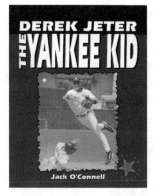

Derek Jeter: The Yankee Kid

Author: Jack O'Connell
ISBN: 1-58261-043-6

In 1996 Derek burst onto the scene as one of the most promising young shortstops to hit the big leagues in a long time. His hitting prowess and ability to turn the double play have definitely fulfilled the early predictions of greatness.

A native of Kalamazoo, MI, Jeter has remained well grounded. He patiently signs autographs and takes time to talk to the young fans who will be eager to read more about him in this book.

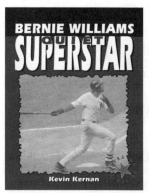

Bernie Williams: Quiet Superstar

Author: Kevin Kernan
ISBN: 1-58261-044-4

Bernie Williams, a guitar-strumming native of Puerto Rico, is not only popular with his teammates, but is considered by top team officials to be the heir to DiMaggio and Mantle fame.

He draws frequent comparisons to Roberto Clemente, perhaps the greatest player ever from Puerto Rico. Like Clemente, Williams is humble, unassuming, and carries himself with quiet dignity. Also like Clemente, he plays with rare determination and a special elegance. He's married, and serves as a role model not only for his three children, but for his young fans here and in Puerto Rico.

Ken Griffey, Jr.: The Home Run Kid

Author: Larry Stone
ISBN: 1-58261-041-x

Capable of hitting majestic home runs, making breathtaking catches, and speeding around the bases to beat the tag by a split second, Ken Griffey, Jr. is baseball's Michael Jordan. Amazingly, Ken reached the Major Leagues at age 19, made his first All-Star team at 20, and produced his first 100 RBI season at 21.

The son of Ken Griffey, Sr., Ken is part of the only father-son combination to play in the same outfield together in the same game, and, like Barry Bonds, he's a famous son who turned out to be a better player than his father.

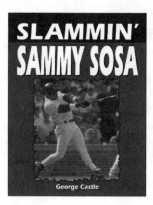

Sammy Sosa: Slammin' Sammy

Author: George Castle
ISBN: 1-58261-029-0

1998 was a break-out year for Sammy as he amassed 66 home runs, led the Chicago Cubs into the playoffs and finished the year with baseball's ultimate individual honor, MVP.

When the national spotlight was shone on Sammy during his home run chase with Mark McGwire, America got to see what a special person he is. His infectious good humor and kind heart have made him a role model across the country.

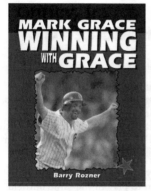

Mark Grace:
Winning with Grace
Author: Barry Rozner
ISBN: 1-58261-056-8

This southern California native and San Diego State alumnus has been playing baseball in the windy city for nearly fifteen years. Apparently the cold hasn't affected his game. Mark is an all-around player who can hit to all fields and play great defense.

Mark's outgoing personality has allowed him to evolve into one of Chicago's favorite sons. He is also community minded and some of his favorite charities include the Leukemia Society of America and Easter Seals.

Randy Johnson:
Arizona Heat!
Author: Larry Stone
ISBN: 1-58261-042-8

One of the hardest throwing pitchers in the Major Leagues, and, at 6'10" the tallest, the towering figure of Randy Johnson on the mound is an imposing sight which strikes fear into the hearts of even the most determined opposing batters.

Perhaps the most amazing thing about Randy is his consistency in recording strikeouts. He is one of only four pitchers to lead the league in strikeouts for four consecutive seasons. With his recent signing with the Diamondbacks, his career has been rejuvenated and he shows no signs of slowing down.

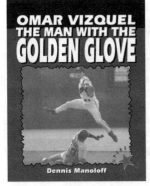

Omar Vizquel: The Man with the Golden Glove
Author: Dennis Manoloff
ISBN: 1-58261-045-2

Omar has a career fielding percentage of .982 which is the highest career fielding percentage for any shortstop with at least 1,000 games played.

Omar is a long way from his hometown of Caracas, Venezuela, but his talents as a shortstop put him at an even greater distance from his peers while he is on the field.

Vizquel resides in Bellevue, Washington with his wife and child.

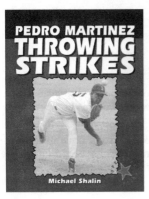

Pedro Martinez: Throwing Strikes
Author: Michael Shalin
ISBN: 1-58261-047-9

The 1997 National League Cy Young Award winner is always teased because of his boyish looks. He's sometimes mistaken for the batboy, but his curve ball and slider leave little doubt that he's one of the premier pitchers in the American League.

It is fitting that Martinez is pitching in Boston, where the passion for baseball runs as high as it does in his native Dominican Republic.

Nomar Garciaparra: High 5!
Author: Michael Shalin
ISBN: 1-58261-053-3

An All-American at Georgia Tech, a star on the 1992 U.S. Olympic Team, the twelfth overall pick in the 1994 draft, and the 1997 American League Rookie of the Year, Garciaparra has exemplified excellence on every level.

At shortstop, he'll glide deep into the hole, stab a sharply hit grounder, then throw out an opponent on the run. At the plate, he'll uncoil his body and deliver a clutch double or game-winning homer. Nomar is one of the game's most complete players.

Juan Gonzalez: Juan Gone!
Author: Evan Grant
ISBN: 1-58261-048-7

One of the most prodigious and feared sluggers in the major leagues, Gonzalez was a two-time home run king by the time he was 24 years old.

After having something of a personal crisis in 1996, the Puerto Rican redirected his priorities and now says baseball is the third most important thing in his life after God and family.

Mo Vaughn:
Angel on a Mission
Author: Michael Shalin
ISBN: 1-58261-046-0

Growing up in Connecticut, this Angels slugger learned the difference between right and wrong and the value of honesty and integrity from his parents early on, lessons that have stayed with him his whole life.

This former American League MVP was so active in Boston charities and youth programs that he quickly became one of the most popular players ever to don the Red Sox uniform.

Mo will be a welcome addition to the Angels line-up and the Anaheim community.

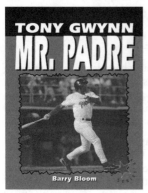

Tony Gwynn:
Mr. Padre
Author: Barry Bloom
ISBN: 1-58261-049-5

Tony is regarded as one of the greatest hitters of all-time. He is one of only three hitters in baseball history to win eight batting titles (the others: Ty Cobb and Honus Wagner).

In 1995 he won the Branch Rickey Award for Community Service by a major leaguer. He is unfailingly humble and always accessible, and he holds the game in deep respect. A throwback to an earlier era, Gwynn makes hitting look effortless, but no one works harder at his craft.

Kevin Brown:
That's Kevin with a "K"
Author: Jacqueline Salman
ISBN: 1-58261-050-9

Kevin was born in McIntyre, Georgia and played college baseball for Georgia Tech. Since then he has become one of baseball's most dominant pitchers and when on top of his game, he is virtually unhittable.

Kevin transformed the Florida Marlins and San Diego Padres into World Series contenders in consecutive seasons, and now he takes his winning attitude and talent to the Los Angeles Dodgers.

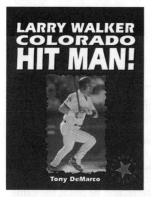

Larry Walker:
Colorado Hit Man!
Author: Tony DeMarco
ISBN: 1-58261-052-5

Growing up in Canada, Larry had his sights set on being a hockey player. He was a skater, not a slugger, but when a junior league hockey coach left him off the team in favor of his nephew, it was hockey's loss and baseball's gain.

Although the Rockies' star is known mostly for his hitting, he has won three Gold Glove awards, and has worked hard to turn himself into a complete, all-around ballplayer. Larry became the first Canadian to win the MVP award.

SUPERSTAR SERIES

Sandy and Roberto Alomar: Baseball Brothers

Author: Barry Bloom
ISBN: 1-58261-054-1

Sandy and Roberto Alomar are not just famous baseball brothers they are also famous baseball sons. Sandy Alomar, Sr. played in the major leagues fourteen seasons and later went into management. His two baseball sons have made names for themselves and have appeared in multiple All-Star games.

With Roberto joining Sandy in Cleveland, the Indians look to be a front-running contender the American League Central.

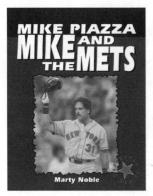

Mike Piazza: Mike and the Mets

Author: Marty Noble
ISBN: 1-58261-051-7

A total of 1,389 players were selected ahead of Mike Piazza in the 1988 draft, who wasn't picked until the 62nd round, and then only because Tommy Lasorda urged the Dodgers to take him as a favor to his friend Vince Piazza, Mike's father.

Named in the same breath with great catchers of another era like Bench, Dickey and Berra, Mike has proved the validity of his father's constant reminder "If you work hard, dreams do come true."

SUPERSTAR SERIES

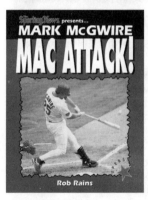

Curt Schilling: Phillie Phire!
Author: Paul Hagen
ISBN: 1-58261-055-x

Born in Anchorage, Alaska, Schilling has found a warm reception from the Philadelphia Phillies faithful. He has amassed 300+ strikeouts in the past two seasons and even holds the National League record for most strikeouts by a right handed pitcher at 319.

This book tells of the difficulties Curt faced being traded several times as a young player, and how he has been able to deal with off-the-field problems.

Mark McGwire: Mac Attack!
Author: Rob Rains
ISBN: 1-58261-004-5

Mac Attack! describes how McGwire overcame poor eyesight and various injuries to become one of the most revered hitters in baseball today. He quickly has become a legendary figure in St. Louis, the home to baseball legends such as Stan Musial, Lou Brock, Bob Gibson, Red Schoendienst and Ozzie Smith. McGwire thought about being a police officer growing up, but he hit a home run in his first Little League at-bat and the rest is history.

Roger Clemens: Rocket Man!
Author: Kevin Kernan
ISBN: 1-58261-128-9

Alex Rodriguez: A-plus Shortstop
ISBN: 1-58261-104-1

SUPERSTAR SERIES

Collect Them All!

____ Sandy and Roberto Alomar:
Baseball Brothers

____ Kevin Brown: Kevin with a "K"

____ Roger Clemens: Rocket Man!

____ Juan Gonzalez: Juan Gone!

____ Mark Grace: Winning With Grace

____ Ken Griffey, Jr.: The Home Run Kid

____ Tony Gwynn: Mr. Padre

____ Derek Jeter: The Yankee Kid

____ Randy Johnson: Arizona Heat!

____ Pedro Martinez: Throwing Strikes

____ Mike Piazza: Mike and the Mets

____ Alex Rodriguez: A-plus Shortstop

____ Curt Schilling: Philly Phire!

____ Sammy Sosa: Slammin' Sammy

____ Mo Vaughn: Angel on a Mission

____ Omar Vizquel:
The Man with a Golden Glove

____ Larry Walker: Colorado Hit Man!

____ Bernie Williams: Quiet Superstar

____ Mark McGwire: Mac Attack!

SP
SPORTS
PUBLISHING
INC.

Available by calling 877-424-BOOK